Guillotine

By January Black.

ISBN#: 978-195534-288-9

Published and curated by:
Iijima Press, in partnership with Holon Publishing

Holon Publishing & Collective Press
A Storytelling Company
www.Holon.co

Printed in the United States of America

IIJIMA
press

Guillotine

January Black.

For Conner and for Trey,
may we never forget to make the call.

Hard to kill.

"

All we can really do is make the Reaper's job hell,
you know? That's what I wish for you, for me, for
anyone. To make the sonofabitch curse your name
as he drags you to hell. To make him swing a few
times. To whiff a few more. To throw out his shoul-
der. To throw out his back. To get his neck out of
whack. To piss blood. To swallow blood. To vomit
blood. To call in the heavies. To let loose the hell-
hounds. To swap out his scythe for a Colt 45. I want
you to be so hard to kill that you get the mother
fucker in serious trouble with his employer. I want
the thought of you to make him lose his erection.
That's it, kid. That's it. I want him to walk into the
bedroom with his mistress, his cloak tattered, his
spirit tattered, his day tattered and I want him to go
limp at the thought of you still living, still breath-
ing, still carrying on. What a glorious, thunderous
way to live. To single-handedly ruin the reaper's sex
life at your outright refusal to die...

"

Your outright refusal to die.

Less hair.
More wrinkles.
Still pretty.
Prettier,
in good lighting,
hiding,
behind a black and white filter.

More words.
More readers.
Seventy-something countries.
Where's Bosnia and Herzegovina?
Are the women pretty there?
The women are pretty everywhere.

Fucking more.
Writing more.
Drinking more.
Wine.
Whiskey.
Coffee.
Too much coffee.
Coffee in the morning.
Coffee in the evening.
Coffee in the afternoon.

Not smiling.

Whitening,
the facades of my teeth
so the coffee doesn't stick.
Still not over my grandmama
getting sick.
Still pretending off-line
I'm Sinatra-slick.
Still selling my soul
to get a fucking click.
Still trying like hell
not to think about my dick.

Coming too fast,
my balls
and my career.
Busting,
breaking,
beneath the weight of this character
I've been creating,
hunchbacked,
in coffee shops in Indiana,
in Tennessee,
in Illinois,
in Colorado.

Lucid
then
Honey Moon
then
Penny Lane
then

Steadfast
then
Ugly Mugs
then
Retrograde
then
Kettner
then
Intelligentsia
then
Passion House
then
Ipsento 606
then
Black Eye

— fuck.

No more mountains.
No more girl.
Raining,
for a little while.
Raining,
for a while.

Then came June,
a black and white nightmare
turned daydream.

Believing more,
in God,

because he put in angel
in a kennel
when my world was catching fire.

My God's different,
though.

He chain-smokes cigarettes.
He has worn hands
like my grandfather's.
He has a heart like my grandmothers.
He has deep cracks in his face
where rivers run through
and eyes that house the world's oceans.
He's as good-looking as Brando.
He's as well-dressed as Flacko.

He can fly
but he prefers to walk.

We talk best over whiskey
and I want to thank him,
you know,
for letting me live another year.

And,
I want to tell him:

Let Hemingway know
I'm coming for him.

Let Hemingway know I'm coming for him.

"

Most men don't have it. I'm not most men. So I will
explain it for these men so they may have it for a
moment, so they know they don't want it, so they
know it isn't good. It's an obsession. It's more than
an obsession. It's an addiction you can't quit with
no amount of rehab. You can take breaks of course.
You can try. You can foolishly try to take breaks, to
walk away, to close up shop. But when you're away
from it you can't stop thinking about it and this is
just the way it is. You want it more than anything:
women, drugs, alcohol, love, kids, wealth, fame.
You want it the same way a dying man wants to do
it all again. You want it the same way a starving man
wants to break bread. You're willing to gamble it all.
Everything. Nothing is safe: your sanity isn't safe,
your legacy isn't safe, your pride isn't safe, your life
isn't safe, your love isn't safe, your religion isn't safe.
You walk down the streets and the world looks at
you differently. They can't keep their eyes off of you,
gazing mixed gazes of fascination and pity, recog-
nizing you for what you really are... a man killing
himself for a muse nobody can see.

"

A man killing himself for a muse nobody can see.

She shows up.
She's naked.
I tell her we got in a fight
and I need a distraction.
She says nothing.
She never says anything.
She just exists with that way
she has of existing.
So elegantly.
So silently.
So wildly.
She lays me down
and kisses my forehead
with her pretty lips.
She makes me feel
like a king.
I am a king.
When we're done
she pulls a cigarette
from her purse
and she smokes it
like it's not killing her.
It can't kill her.
She's alive for as long as I am.
She dies when I do.
When she moves to her
second cigarette

she points to
the typewriter
on my desk next to the books
and the plants.
It's black as night.
She is
silently telling me to sit down.
I listen.
I start typing.
She keeps smoking.
The next morning,
she's nowhere to be found,

but she left me these pages.

But she left me these pages.

You walk into Folk with your folks
letting in a summer breeze
I want to dive into
like those lakes that festoon
the face of Southern Indiana
with wet kisses.

Eventually,
you turn and you look my way
and we hold each other
for a James Blunt moment.

My homie stops the music,
whispering something about who you are,
whispering something about not staring
(because of who you are).

And then as if God hears his words
and is enticed to test my will,
the host seats you at the table
directly across from me
and for the rest of the night
you are the Sun.

You are the Sun
I won't allow myself to look at.

You are the Sun
I see but only in glances
I collect like daisies
and lilacs and wild azaleas
to make this bouquet
I'm writing now,
this bouquet that I will press
in-between the pages of a book
you will never read.

You are the Sun
I can't reach out and touch
but that I can feel warming me
and the people in this room.

You are the Sun
I want to bottle up and swallow
and get drunk on,
intoxicated off the possibility
of you becoming
something so much more than
the Sun across the room.

The sun across the room.

I'm standing in the kitchen

with my back against the island,

wincing down an eyeballed Negroni

(that tastes like an eyeballed Negroni)

as I rob glances at you

standing outside on the patio,

letting the moon paint your face.

Fancy says something gloriously funny

and you throw back your head in laughter.

Your mouth is open,

as if you are a child

and the stars have turned to flakes of snow.

The stars have turned to flakes of snow.

She's somewhere. It's snowing. She's sipping
on something. She's window shopping, steal-
ing glances inside warm, illuminated buildings
housing gift stores and coffee shops and bars and
restaurants serving up expensive steaks and bot-
tles of wine to match.

Beside her there is a man — there is always a man
beside the woman you want — they've been togeth-
er for a great while, you can see it in the way they
exist in this foreign place as if there is an invisible
string holding the two of them together. She goes
and he follows. He goes and she follows. It is both
beautiful and nauseating, all at the same time.

I'm walking seventeen long strides behind them,
my battered red wings crushing the snow beneath
their soles — soles whose grip has been smoothed to
marble at the hands of the rough unforgiving terrain
of Belarus and Chicago and later Colorado — I slip
every now and again, sometimes catching myself,
sometimes not, never taking my gaze off of them.

She's bouncing, like a slow-moving pinball, in-be-
tween his heavy outstretched arm and the windows
that look like passing train cars in the falling winter.

Every few windows something will catch her eyes, drawing her near and away from him, with her mittened hands she will coax him to come hither, pulling the string, begging him to take in this ordinary thing that when witnessed together, for whatever reason, makes it extraordinary — this is love, I write down behind my watchful eyes, being with someone that makes our very ordinary existences feel like something extraordinary.

With each stop, I stop, scared they will turn around and see me, mistaking me for a stalker and not a writer gathering material for the piece you're reading now.

They linger, for a long while, in front of the window of this cafe where lazy felines lie in small, slowly breathing heaps. She points at one of these heaps that closely resembles their great tri-colored Maine Coon, waiting for them at home.

The man isn't looking at the cat, he's looking at her looking at the cat. He can't take his eyes off of her. *Jesus Christ, please, take your eyes off of her.*

The couple, they're on the move again, he always on the right side of her subconsciously buffering her from the passing cars. I strangely feel comforted by this, knowing she's okay, knowing she's protected, knowing he's forever looking after her as long as he's breathing — but, this comfort is frozen and then shattered with the hammer that is him stopping, turning, facing her, underneath this street light that shines down as if heaven has opened its windows and God is watching.

He gets down on one knee. His tall frame shrinking to nothing. He pulls off his gloves, reaching for a bulge in the back pocket of his jeans. Out from its depths, he unveils a box that kills him, that kills me, watching from afar. He's saying something. I'm squinting trying desperately to read his lips. I can't look away.

She's standing over him, her mittened hands close to her face in disbelief, behind her beating heart she feels her soul for the first time. Her shaking hands rip off the mittens covering them. She's so warm she can't feel them freezing, she can't feel them growing numb. All she can do is nod, over and over and over again, as if she is falling into a dream.

He slips a ring on her finger, holds her hands in his, warming them between his, kissing them, water in his eyes, trailing down, turning to ice, smiling, breaking the ice, crying some more. He collapses, his face and his head and his heart and his soul into her belly, his arms wrapped around her waist, his knees kissing the ground, she's holding his head close to her body, her face is a beautiful wreck.

And, I watch on, from afar, in the alley, the heat
from my cigarette won't let the water in my eyes
turn to ice, staring at you and staring at me and
staring at this distant dream of what you and I
could have been.

When I've finally had enough, I blink long and hard
as if to seal my eyelids shut and when I open them
we are gone.

I ice the cigarette, I slide my hands into my pockets
and I walk up to the single beam shining down on the
white pavement and I look up, at the falling snow, at
the light, at the dark starry night sky and I swear I
see God, asking me if I'm ready to come home.

God, asking me if I'm ready to come home.

I reach for the Klonopin.

I swallow the first and the second,
I chew the third and the fourth,
I crush the rest into a white line
and I breathe.

My breathing slows, slower,
slower even

and I drift off.

I'm gone.

I open my eyes in a white room
with bad lighting,

the kind of

lighting

that turns your skin jaundiced.

God is at his desk.

He's smoking

an American Spirit,

brooding

behind a plume of smoke.

All I can see is his eyes,
his beautiful fucking eyes,
his beautiful fucking jaguar eyes
ready to lurch out and kill me,

again.

Instead, he stands up,
steps through the tremendous smoke,
kisses me on my forehead,

ashes out his cigarette
between

my eyes
and tells me:

he has run out of rooms.

He has run out of rooms.

The blades of your shoulders are biting into the bed
as its sheets and covers and pillows tangle around you.

You're still.

Your stillness and the linen's affection for your flesh
remind me of the stone angels
that sit outside the homes of the old rich
screaming out as the vines of the abandoned landscape
drag them to hell.

I grab you by your wrists and I stretch out your arms,
turning them to wings as I whisper in your ear to lie still.

You're splayed.
You're Christ, crucified.

And I'm looking at you with the same eyes
as the saints and the angels do God
as they witness God be God
in all those famous paintings.

If Jesus Christ had a body as divine as yours,
these Christians would be masturbating in church.

I worship you,

pressing my lips to yours
and gently holding your chin;

as my hands move down to your neck
and to your chest
and finally towards your hips
where I war with the temptation
of driving my nails through your skin
as if your soul resides in there,

somewhere.

I bite and teethe and suck at your breasts
like a man-child
hugged to the bosom of Aphrodite,
reminding myself this isn't the final destination,
that I can't remain here,
that I can't build my home here,
that I can't stop

— not here.

my lips walk my face and my head and my mind
and my heart down to the space between your legs
where your pussy is snow,
melting to wet at the touch of my tongue
and my fingertips

— fingertips

I eventually slide into you
and reach skyward,
as if I'm lunging for the hand of God.

I strum and I pluck and I dance inside of you
until we arrive at this place,
this beautiful place
where your voice goes from song to silence,
to this place where you can't seem to find the words
nor the breath,

and in this place,
I wonder to myself if men were wrong —

if heaven is not here.

If heaven is not here.

Two chairs with her have a way of becoming one.

One drink with her has a way of becoming two.

An evening with her has a way of becoming morning.

Breakfast with her has a way of becoming heaven.

Heaven without her has a way of becoming hell.

Hell with her has a way of becoming possible.

A weekend away from her has a way of becoming an eternity.

An eternity with her has a way of becoming a ball

— a ball you never want to drop.

A ball you never want to drop.

Out the window, I spy the plane's left wing
wiggling like a loose tooth.

I can't stare, not for too long,
otherwise my stomach eats itself
like a frightened animal
that has bounded into the forest
right into the open mouth
of a bear trap.

I can't stare, not for too long,
otherwise black-widowed visions
of sputtering engines and black smoke
turn to cancer in my mind.

I can't stare, not for too long,
otherwise I lie awake
with red eyes on this red-eye,
knifing myself bloody with all the things
I should have said to you
before my jet ate the ground.

Before my jet ate the ground.

You dream when you're dead. They never tell you that. When you're dead and you fall into sleep, dreaming feels like a dream within a dream.

I know this cannot make any sort of sense. Not to you, because you're not yet dead. Hold onto the sentiment, though, for that fateful day the black-hooded man arrives at your door and whisks you away.

Once on the other side, you will inevitably find yourself sleeping and then dreaming and this dreaming will feel like swimming in water beneath water.

Then, when you wake, breaching the surface of the dream like some great whale, shaking away the evening cold, you will still be cold, because you are dead after all, but you will just find that you are met with a different kind of cold, a forever cold, rather than a sharp cold that takes your breath away.

This is the worst part of being dead; this forever cold. I loathe it. I can't seem to get warm. Lately, I've been dreaming about this moment with my wife, a moment that happened every morning over the decade we spent together. The dream goes something like this...

"

It's early. The two of us have gone from sleeping to only half so. We're shaken into consciousness by stripes. Red stripes. Yellow stripes. Orange stripes.

It's the sun. It's lonely. It's longing for company. And, it's demanding this company, our company, by squirming like a snake in between the spaces of our bedroom blinds. It's the sun whispering warm zebra stripes on our hardwood floors and on the covers that hold us.

Her eyes are closed. She's lying on her side, facing me, our legs are intertwined. She searches for my hand with her own. It reminds me of a lazy, sleepy octopus, turning over rocks, looking for something it had lost in the nighttime.

I stretch my arm out, helping her in her search. Our hands meet, our fingers intertwine and she asks me the question she'd ask me every morning for as long as I knew her: *What did you dream about?*

I begin spilling out the contents of my dream: the places I went, the people I saw, the experiences that might be worthy of writing about.

She'd never open her eyes through any of this retelling. She'd just listen, so intently, her smile turning gently skyward when she found something I had dreamt amusing. And, in the mornings, when the dreams weren't dreams but terrors, she'd squeeze my hand with hers, letting me know she was there, the entire time — if not in the dream, beside me, through the night.

And in the nightmares that followed the mornings of these dreams, she'd always say to me, promise me, that my dreams would be much sweeter.

And they always were. They always were sweeter.

"

Nowadays, now on the other side, I still sleep beside her. Only now she doesn't know it. She can only get a sense of it, from time to time. She will wake up and she will frantically reach out, looking for my hand and I will frantically reach back — trying desperately to make contact, to touch her, to feel her, to help her in her search, to feel her skin again.

Her hand will finally settle as she realizes I'm not there, that I haven't been for some time.

But, I am here, baby. I am here. I have been here since the day those oncoming headlights caught us like hungry sharks.

And what they don't tell you about being dead is
that your dreams are your heaven and the angels you
once loved are the victims that you haunt.

Sleep well, my love.

Sleep well, my love.

You're not sleepy? What? You want to hear the mountain story? Baby, you've heard that story so many times. Okay. Okay.

Once upon a time there was a boy who fell for a princess who lived atop a great mountain...

You have to tuck in Mr. Bear? Okay, tuck him in. Yes. He looks warm. Yes. You do take such good care of him, sweetie...

Once upon a time there was a boy who fell in love with a princess who lived atop a great mountain. The boy stood at the foot of this mountain and shouted up, as loud as he could, trying to get her attention, trying to get her to look his way.

Eventually, she heard him and looked down with eyes like forests. She asked the boy what he wanted and the boy said "her" and "for her to go with him, to his home".

But the princess's home was on the mountain and she told the boy the only way she'd go is if she could take her mountain with her.

And so the boy put his back up against this great mountain and dug his heels into the dirt and begun to push and push and push —

Well, that didn't take long...

Goodnight, dove.

Goodnight, dove.

I killed her, yesterday. She's still alive and breathing,
somewhere, with someone that isn't me, whispering
the same lovely lines in his ears she once did in mine.

I killed her, yesterday. And after three, maybe four
years, I finally found it within myself to go back,
to go back to the very place she and I would spend
our days together, that tiny beach town with the
sand, white like cocaine, and the water, an unbe-
lievable blue.

I killed her, yesterday. I packed up my beat-up land
cruiser as if she were right there with me, guiding
my hand. I packed the frozen cherries she'd pop
in her mouth, turning them to slush. I packed
the marinated scallops she adored to cook on
the beach, to the setting sun, over an open fire. I
packed the bourbon and made sure it was good and
it was chill, just how she liked it. I packed the mar-
ijuana, the hearty hard-hitting shit, enough to get
Marley to the moon and back. I packed her thick
bohemian blanket, still riddled with sand from our
previous trip, our last adventure. I packed the beat-
up boombox and the busted-up lawn chairs and the
tattered tent that let you steal slivers of the stars.

I killed her, yesterday. I fired up my Toyota and I raced down I-65, fighting the urge not to eat the gun in my glove compartment, painting the inside of my car the same crimson red she used to paint her fingernails.

I killed her, yesterday. I arrived, cold, the dead of winter. I set up the campsite high up on the beach, high enough to dodge the tide, just as she taught me, just as we had done so many times before. I kicked on the boombox and I scoured the shore for driftwood, the ocean had grown bored of.

I killed her, yesterday. I set the wood ablaze. I ate the cherries as I cooked the scallops and washed them both down with the good, chilled bourbon. Then, I smoked as I watched the sun abandon the sky and tuck itself in, beneath the ocean.

I killed her, yesterday. Once the sun was finished with her show, I watched the fire smolder into nothing. And once to nothing, she finally appeared, a ghost in the night, a ghost from a past life. She crept up from the ocean, a mermaid sprouting legs, and made her way over to me with her long generous stride.

I killed her, yesterday. Closer, ever closer, she fell down, onto her knees and then began to crawl, like a dying lioness. Into the tattered tent she went and into the tattered tent I followed. Inside, we existed in a new world, a starcraft floating through time and space, looking up at the moon through its bullet soaked windshield.

I killed her, yesterday. I kissed her, lightly, on the lips and then I told her I was sorry, that I must finally let her go.

I must finally let her go.

"

You worry about her the same way you worry about the women that came before her. But, she's young and she's been kissed by the sun and her hair is honey and she's got oceans churning in the whites of her eyes and she's going to find a man, a good man, a man that'll put you to rest, a man that'll erase your touch, a man that'll salt the places you've kissed, a man that'll make you as pretty as an after-thought — and all I hope is that when this man does show, you love her enough not to pick up the phone —

"

You love her enough not to pick up the phone.

He finds her outside,
barefoot,
on her balcony,
eyeing a moon so big and so bright
you'd believe it had inched closer
sometime in the night.

She feels him behind her
and she leans back
knowing his chest will catch her.

She's quiet.
He's quiet.
The world is quiet.
So quiet he can hear her mind
spooning thoughts into her mouth
like a worried mother.

Thoughts she's trying not to swallow.
Thoughts she finally spits out...

She says she thinks they should have a sign,
if he ever goes before her.

She says that if he comes to visit,
she wants to know not to shoo him away,
to ask him to stay,

to keep him coming back,
again and again,
to hold him close,
on this side,

or the other.

On this side, or the other.

While I love that tall dark hair of yours,
I'll love you when it frays.

While I love those wet hazelnut eyes of yours,
I'll love you when time paints them grey.

While I love that soft behind of yours,
I'll love you when it changes shape.

While I love the way you whisper my name,
I'll love you the day my name escapes.

While I love that smooth skin of yours,
I'll love you when time leaves her marks.

While I love that gorgeous mind of yours,
I'll love you when it's swimming with sharks.

While I love the way you look my way,
I'll love you when you're upset and won't.

While I love the mornings we wake up together,
please know I'll love you the day we don't.

I'll love you the day we don't.

I knew I wanted her to be the mother of my children long before she knew she wanted to and long before it would have been even remotely acceptable to inform her of this desire.

We were sitting in her car in the dead of winter eating soft-serve ice cream, the heat was blazing, warming our bodies, while we chilled our mouths with each passing bite.

Right after I had taken in a big scoop of soft serve, she reached her face across the center console and pressed her lips to mine and then she smiled as she went back to eating her ice cream, leaving me with frozen butterflies, thawing out in my stomach.

She said, *You're a healthy puppy.*

I shot her a bewildered look and she took note of my bewilderment and continued, *My momma would say that to me when I'd come in from the snow. My nose would be wet and freezing and she'd kiss it as she unbundled me and she'd say, "Did you know healthy puppies have wet, cold snouts?" You're a healthy puppy.*

It was the prettiest thing I had ever heard and in that moment I knew it was something I wanted her to say to my children, our children, one day, when they came in from playing in the cold with noses and mouths as cold as icicles.

And as I was having this thought she leaned over, once again, and kissed me on my lips, *You're a healthy puppy.*

Unfortunately, we never got that chance. I will tell you why. But, you have to promise to believe me. Do you promise to believe me?

You see, Evelyn was different. Evelyn was a witch. Not a bad witch. A good witch. The kind of witch you want around, every moment of every day. This is the problem with good witches, you fall in love with them and you can't imagine life without them and then one day, they must go.

God or the universe gave her this strange ability.

She had 100 years to live and she could stretch these 100 years to an eternity. She could add a year to her life if she removed a year from a human she crossed paths with. She didn't have to know them nor touch them nor speak to them.

She just had to look in their direction and the exchange could be made. They would live one year less and she would live one year more.

The caveat, however, was that this power worked both ways. She could remove a year from her own life and gift it to someone else.

So you can imagine, when she told me this, I thought she was crazy. Truly crazy. But then one day, we were on the CTA rocketing for downtown when she looked at this elderly gentleman.

He was smiling. He was smiling at this tiny little girl who was sitting on his lap, grabbing his great big nose and hugging him and calling him *papa*.

Evelyn looked at the elderly man in a way I had never seen anyone look at anyone before. And in a blink of an eye, he looked younger. Not just by a year but by a decade.

One moment he was 70 and the next moment he looked something like 60 and while he didn't notice a thing, his granddaughter did. She gave him a peculiar look, only for a moment, straining to recognize him.

Then, she went back to playing, jumping up and down and grabbing his (still) great big nose.

I looked at Evelyn and she just looked out the window of the CTA like nothing had happened.

Later that day I asked her how many years she had left.

To which she looked at me, this time without a smile, *one.*

She was twenty-four.

That evening I asked her to take a decade off mine.

She said no.

I asked her to take years off mine.

She said no.

I asked her to take a year off mine.

She said no.

And, the two of us got into the worst fight we had ever been in. We screamed and we shouted and we cursed at one another and I told her how selfish she was for doing this to me; to us.

And then, I started crying, uncontrollably. I couldn't stop and I just fell into her and she held me and she cried too and in between sobs I asked her why and she said, *Because some lives need a little bit longer than others to leave this world better than they found it.*

That night, I made her promise me that moment on the CTA would be her last. That she would, at the very least, give us this one last year.

That night, she made me this promise. And, for the next year, I never let Evelyn go. I loved her harder than I had ever loved anyone or anything in my life. And, I tried desperately not to count down the days, not to watch the calendar, the clock.

But, in the backs of our minds we knew the end was approaching, little by little, nearing in like the tide.

One evening, we found ourselves once again, in her car in the dead of winter with the heat on high and the windows fogging up, eating ice cream, she reached over and pressed her lips against mine and said, *You're a healthy puppy.*

And, she was gone.

It's been four decades. I have a wife who I love dearly who isn't Evelyn and I have three beautiful daughters I love desperately, who aren't Evelyn's. The last of which, I will be walking down the aisle, today.

I have something growing in my chest that my doctor says will kill me. He says to rest easy on this day, though.

To enjoy it.

To be here for it.

He says I still have a year.

He says I still have a year.

I'ma

get loaded off a fifth of Buffalo Trace

and
I'ma

go hunting for a guillotine.

I'ma high-tail it
out to the backroads
that run through Southern Indiana

like asphalt rivers.

I'ma
row those rivers,

faster,
ever faster.

I'ma lose control.

I'ma wrap my '89

around the trunk
of a big 'ole sycamore.

The trunk of a big 'ole sycamore.

There is a polaroid of her
on the dashboard of my '89 Range Rover;

a polaroid where she's bending the wind
with an oriental fan;

as she gazes over her left shoulder,
her eyes devouring something the camera cannot see;

I can see her now,
standing still in a bed of dust
the sun has turned to dandelions;

it's as if she's staring at my speedometer,
coaxing me to drive faster to her;

to slow down for her.

To slow down for her.

Candles

are burning their tiny worlds to nothing

in the dark of my room;

darkness that's turning her brown hair black;

black that she's tied up in a mess

that hangs high above her head like an angel

trying to hide her halo.

She's naked from head to toe.

She's naked

save for a vintage black Boondock Saints t-shirt

that clings to her

like my grandmother's kimono.

Like my grandmother's kimono.

Last night I dreamed I was tasked with putting a
bullet in Saddam Hussein's head.

So, I snuck into my grandfather's home and I got my
hands on his hunting rifle stowed away in the back of
his closet behind the piled boxes of my dead grand-
mother's purses and shoes.

I grabbed it and began digging through those boxes
and somewhere inside one of her purses was enough
ammunition to turn a grizzly into Swiss cheese.

Loaded for bear, I caught a Southwest flight to Iraq.

They let me take the gun on the flight because every-
body knew what I was tasked with and the Southwest
flight flew direct and arrived in an hour because it
was a dream and planes can do that in dreams.

When I arrived at the great gates guarding his estate,
they swung open as if Hussein was expecting me.

I walked into the den of the dragon, my red wings
cracking pepper as they dug into the chat that made
up his driveway.

I would have thought this dictator could afford pavement.

Eventually, I found him smoking a great cigar, around back, seated on the edge of his swimming pool. He looked up at me, seeing me and the gun and seeing what I was to do.

He waved his hand in a come hither motion, ready to shake hands with his fate, as I shot him between the eyes.

And for a split second I saw both eyes widen and turn out as his brain and his skull and his head expanded. As he became two, the world filled the space where he was once one.

It was in this space where I saw the bullet had ripped through him and tore into the belly of a small girl in the water behind him.

It took me a moment to see that it was more than a small girl, that it was my best friend's daughter.

The water turned a deep red as she played and she swam, not realizing what had happened.

And I just stared at her, the soles of my red wings like a pair of great whites in the pooling blood of Sudaam Hussein.

I knew she was going to die.

But, a part of me felt that if I didn't move the bleeding would stop.

And when I woke up the next morning, my best friend wrote to me on a glowing screen, telling me the doctor had called and the pain in his daughter's belly was now breaking his heart.

And I just lied there, not moving a muscle.

And I just lied there, not moving a muscle.

After they fucked,
he never knew what to say.

He could ask her if it was good,
but he knew if he had to ask,
it wasn't.

He could ask her if she came,
but he knew if he had to ask,
she didn't.

So he didn't say anything at all.

He just lied there,
until the lying got cheap.

Until the lying got cheap.

"

You're not a writer unless it hurts more not to write
than to write something bad. You're not a writer
unless your mind never goes quiet, unless you're
exhausted from constantly absorbing everything and
racing to capture everything and filtering out the bad
like scum atop a swimming pool and clenching onto
the good like lost cash found in a pocket that has
missed your hand. You're not a writer unless nothing
is off-limits: no body, no experience, no moment.
You're not a writer if you can turn it on and off like
a light switch. You're not a writer if you'd stop if the
applause stopped. You're not a writer.

"

You're not a writer.

Boy, I don't own no slick 44.
I ain't gonna dig a hole in your head.

I ain't lookin' to even the score
in a dark alleyway with a muzzle full of lead.

I just gotta typewriter, 26 keys to count
and enough dog in me to be heard on the moon.

You keep on howling I'll turn you inside out,
write your demons on these pages, tattered and strewn.

Boy, I don't own no slick 44.
I'ma warm-hearted hoosier, that I am sure.

But, run me too hard and you'll beg like a whore
for some whisky, some Klonopin and a slick 44.

Some whisky, some Klonopin and a slick 44.

Your face is dangerous, baby.
Your face is an accident waiting to happen, baby.
Your face is a head-turner, baby.
Your face is a car wreck, baby.
Your face is a plane crash, baby.
Your face is turbulence in my chest, baby.
Your face is a bottle full of Klonopin, baby.
Your face is a night hang turned red-eye, baby.
Your face is tomorrow's daydream, baby.
Your face is a Tennessee Winehouse, baby.
Your face is the death of a Southern Indiana boy, baby.
Your face is a guillotine, baby.
Your face is a vase full of roses, baby —

dying,
dying,
dying,
dead.

Your face is a vase full of dead roses
I'll never throw away,

baby.

I'll never throw away, baby.

"

It ain't about finding love. It's about giving love a chance. It's about giving love a chance. It's about giving love a chance. You give it a chance and you keep on giving it that chance and eventually you wake up and it feels like it's been there all along. It might be the blonde with the pretty-faced tabby who she can't love on before she comes and loves on you because you'll sneeze until your eyes run red. It might be the redhead turning redder in Oceanside that blames your chemistry on your zodiac signs; that blames your demise on your zodiac signs, too. It might be the brunette with the ocean eyes that spilled out the Atlantic when she found out you were stealing time in Montreal with the gal in the next sentence. It might be the gal who looks like Halsey before Halsey was Halsey, Canadian-born and Canadian-raised, that kisses on your lips like she's tapping for maple syrup. It might be the Christian who has a way of forgetting her religion at the taste of whisky and wine, who always wakes up sober, cursing a devil like you, whispering apologies to Jesus Christ for giving into a devil like you, eventually, forgiving a devil like you, doing it all again with a devil like you. *Run, boy, run. You can't compete with God, boy.* It might be the green-eyed Gemini,

57.

mountainside, who wanted you to stay and leave at the same time, who's a stranger now, who's a child-hood crush again now, who's a 'once upon a time' now, who's a wide-eyed night's sleep now, who's a bottle full of Klonopin now, who's a whiskey-a-night now, who's a two-whiskeys-a-night now, who's a dozen plane tickets collecting dust in the back of your closet now, who's a two-hundred blood-soaked pages of poetry and prose now, whose a cardiac arrest in a Timehop now. It might be the nurse rushing in at the nick of time, stitching you back together again with her manicured hands, pumping your heart back to life again with her manicured hands, begging for the soul you can't give her with her manicured hands.

"

With her manicured hands.

You're nothing but a racehorse,
kid.

They'll love you,
they'll praise you,
they'll respect you,

for as long as you're winning,
for as long as that muse of yours
is riding atop your back,
whispering in your ear.

But as soon as she leaps from your back
and onto the back
of a younger horse
with stronger legs
and a fuller mane,

this ends.

You're a dying man,

you just don't know it yet,
kid.

You just don't know it yet, kid.

He told that boy, judge.
He warned he held a grudge.

But that fool kept on writing her,
wagering his life for another man's wife, sir.

So he dragged the poor bastard by his throat
cold steel, heavy, wintering in his coat.

It was here I heard a wraith from my quiet little boxcar
as he turned him into meat with that violent-looking crowbar.

And once he had his fill, the boy's voice a deathly wail,
he wrapped his bloody lips and teeth around a railroad nail.

Then he kicked him like a snarling dog underneath the chin
the shattering cracked for miles as he lay drowning in his sin.

That boy's been dead many years, some nights I hear him whisper,
the fissures in his teeth now leave that sweet talker a lisper.

He told that boy, judge.
He warned he held a grudge.

But that fool kept on writing her,
wagering his life for another man's wife, sir.

Wagering his life for another man's wife, sir.

Your sweetness hurts like a mouthful of cavities, honey.
Your sweetness hurts like my molars have gone red, honey.
Your sweetness hurts like a fever dream, honey.
Your sweetness hurts like the bottom of a whiskey barrel, honey.
Your sweetness hurts like what could have been, honey.

Your sweetness hurts like the dragons and dreams
that sit in the back of an old man's mind,
smiling their terrible pointed smiles,
reminding him that he almost had them
had he not taken to your sweetness, honey.

Your sweetness is a dream killer, honey.
Your sweetness is a coffin nail, honey.

Your sweetness is a coffin nail, honey.

Southwest, window-side,
watching her watch the world.

She's sitting, cross-legged,
reminding me of that Jason Isbell song
about the elephant...

"... cross-legged on a barstool like nobody sits any-
more..."

The elephant in our room,
in our world,
the one I'm watching her watch
from her cabin window,
is that we're falling for one another
at the same velocity as this 747
tearing through the sky at 500 miles an hour

and neither of us can find the words
to admit it.

Because, maybe,
when you start admitting
to yourself that you're falling,
you open yourself up to the possibility
of getting hurt
— a hurt that looks like

a world
they're no longer a part of;
a world that they're apart from.

The elephant in our room
is that I never want to live in a world
where I look over
and I don't see her
staring out that cabin window,

cross-legged.

Staring out that cabin window, cross-legged.

The flight attendant hands me
a pack of American Airline branded
miniature pretzels and a plastic cup
of lukewarm apple juice
that tastes sweet enough to pour
over a stack of pancakes.

I drop the tiny, salty knots into my mouth
in twos and threes,
untying them with crunching molars
and then washing them down with the syrup.

I think of snack time
back in elementary school,
back when a cup of chocolate pudding
chilled for twenty minutes in the icebox
tasted better than Tiramisu.

Tasted better than Tiramisu.

She's in her kitchen
glued to a hovering island
so big it could be
an ancient UFO.

Beach House echoes
from her living room,

"It was late at night,
you held on tight..."

This spacey symphony
oozes from a glowing screen
mounted in-between two
pristine white couches
so good-looking you'd
never fuck on them.

For some reason,
this atmosphere leaves
me thinking about dying.

I don't want to die.
I don't want her to die, either.

God bless Isbell
but I want to be a vampire.

That or I want to get hit by a bus
before I ever have the chance
to fall —

She turns.
She sees me.

She sees me
as if it's her first time
seeing me.

Her hair is high above her head
in a mess exposing a pair of ears
that can hear melodies the rest
of us can't.

I want to kiss them
and whisper into them
along with the muses
and the angels
that follow her around
like bluebirds
follow bluebirds.

She smiles softly.
Always softly, at first.
Then, she melts
and I along with her.

She walks.
She throws her arms around me.
She leaps.
She wraps her legs around me.
She leans.
She paints her lips all over me.

Later.

Cooking dinner.
Sharing songs like favorite stories.
Sharing stories like favorite songs.
When I'm with her I feel like
I knew her once upon a time
a thousand years ago
and someone killed us
and now the two of us are rushing,
rushing,
rushing,
to catch one another up on
a thousand years of
material.

Later.

Something is hot in the oven.
Smoke.
Her fire alarms blare.
The drums in her ears
can't take it:

laughing,
scrambling,
cursing,
deactivating.

Silence.

Silence.

"

Writer's block isn't all that dissimilar to a bad case
of whiskey dick. After a hard night of drinking,
you and your partner have to leave your pride at
the door, you have to fail a few times, you have to
muster up an awkward laugh or two. But, eventually,
if you keep at it, the two of you will stumble upon a
beautiful breakthrough: hot, inebriated lovemak-
ing at 2 a.m. followed by a pizza or a bowl of Lucky
Charms. And, in the rare cases when these failures
lead to more failures, you're going to get your ass to
bed and try again in the morning (after you make
love to her with your goddamn mouth because
you're a team player and you're not going to pout
just because your coach didn't put you in the game).
This is the only cure for writer's block. You write
your way through it. You write your way through
it. You write your way through it. And, if this still
results in handfuls of shit, you get up, dust yourself
off, down a beer and try again in the morning.

"

Down a beer and try again in the morning.

You don't hate me
because I'm kissing
on the lips
whispering
your favorite melodies.

You hate me
because you see me
smiling in photographs
knowing I never
smile in photographs.

You hate me
because I'm happy.

You hate me
because you don't think I deserve
to be happy.

And, I hate myself
because I don't think I deserve
to be happy, either.

I don't think I deserve to be happy, either.

Yesterday, I went to my friend's daughter's birthday party — who was unapologetically using the celebration as an excuse to get hammered on a Pontoon boat with a bunch of her adult friends.

Being that neither myself nor any of the adults in attendance were owners of a lake-faring vessel, we paid a sixty-something-year-old man who called himself Captain Bill $1,000 to cart us around Old Hickory Lake in Hendersonville, Tennessee as we drank, overate, listened to music and "celebrated" my friend's daughter.

The moment I stepped on board, I could tell Captain Bill was over-qualified for what he had been hired to do — he was dressed in white sailor garb and firmly planted atop his head was what appeared to be a Navy Officer's Cap, which he wore proudly, in much the same way a prized German Shepard wears his ears.

In his right hand, he held a radio transmitter that looked as if it belonged on a naval warcraft, not a rinky-dink Pontoon boat.

Before firing up the engine, he phoned "command" with said radio transmitter, making "the big dogs" aware of he and his crew's departure.

He then gave us a ten-minute rundown of the rules…

The first rule was that we were prohibited to listen to music that used any sort of foul or graphic language.

The second rule was that we couldn't smoke.

While there were a few smokers in attendance, none of them gave Captain Bill any sort of shit for not being allowed to smoke onboard.

But, Captain Bill felt inclined to inform us that not only was smoking on a boat dangerous due to the fumes the engine emits… but that just a week prior, a woman was smoking a cigarette too close to a boat motor, became a human bonfire and was airlifted to a nearby hospital.

Captain Bill hammered in the extent of her injuries by saying…

"She was so badly burned that she probably wishes she were dead."

Upon sharing this detail, you could hear a few of the parents groan a little bit and shift uncomfortably in their seats, glancing in our friend's daughter's direction, making sure she wasn't paying too much attention to Captain Bill's safety briefing.

The third rule was that there was no diving.

Again, nobody argued this rule. But, Captain Bill wanted to be crystal clear. So, he informed us that there was a ten-year-old kid who dove into the lake a few months back in an area he mistakenly thought was shallow and that, because of this mistake, he will never be able to walk again.

At this point, my friend, the mother who had booked Captain Bill for her daughter's birthday yelled...

"Jesus Christ Bill, this is my daughter's birthday party, can you please just give us the rules without all the details?"

With raised eyebrows, perhaps impressed with my friend's feistiness, Captain Bill nodded at her and continued on, mostly unphased, saving us from the specifics but remaining very much long-winded.

While everyone was quite turned off by Captain Bill, I was watering at the mouth — I could tell Captain Bill had seen some shit and didn't contain the kind of filter that would normally keep people who had seen some shit from sharing said shit they had seen (in tremendous and excruciating detail) with nosey writers like myself.

So, once we had anchored in a shady area of the lake, I cornered Captain Bill, making sure children and angry parents were out of earshot and I asked him what he did before he drove Pontoon boats for a living.

I nipped at my glass of tequila as Captain Bill told me that he was a Navy Seal in Vietnam and his job was to kill "double-agents."

He said it wasn't like the James Bond movies — there were no bald-headed villains with eye-patches wielding laser pistols — normally it was someone you thought was working for you but you'd eventually find out was working for the Viet Cong. His job was to make these people disappear.

I didn't ask for specifics on these disappearances.

But, you know Captain Bill...

He told me that one night he was sleeping on an outstretched tree limb when a small troop of Viet Cong soldiers passed underneath him.

Towards the back of the pack, he noticed there was a soldier falling behind.

He patiently waited for him to stumble by and the moment he did, Captain Bill hooked his knees and legs around the tree limb, as you would a set of monkey bars, and silently flipped upside down on the branch like a deranged Spiderman and plunged a large blade in the back of the man's neck near the spine, which he then ran across his jugular and into his windpipe.

Captain Bill then grabbed the soldier by the head, as his blood turned red the forest floor and held him upright to keep him from tumbling and startling the rest of his comrades who were continuing their journey up ahead.

Once the coast was clear, Captain Bill leaped down from the tree. Ripped open the dead soldier's shirt. Carved a large "B" in the man's chest — which he claimed he did to all of his victims — and then he tossed the corpse off to the side of the road. Finally, he high-tailed it in the opposite direction towards his base.

When I say my jaw dropped at the telling of this story, a corporate executive could have smacked golf balls into my mouth on the carpeted floor of his corner office.

As you can imagine, the entire boat trip eventually went to hell in a handbasket.

At one point, it all got so bad that one of the parents called Captain Bill a "fucking piece of shit," which made me feel bad for Captain Bill until I saw how unconcerned he was by the remark.

The parent repeated the insult several times until Captain Bill gave his rebuttal...

"Sir, I've been doing these boat tours for years now and I'll have you know... you're the first party to ever not offer the captain a drink."

It took me a long time to understand what it was that bothered the folks on the Pontoon so much about Captain Bill (besides the fact that Captain Bill was an asshole).

For now, here's my theory...

We don't like thinking about death, nor being reminded that death is a possibility, especially whilst on a Pontoon boat, surrounded by friends, drinking drinks and celebrating young life.

With this, I think that we naturally create distance between ourselves and the people who remind us that it all will eventually end — whether that be in a jungle in Vietnam at the hands of Captain Bill or smoking a cigarette too close to a leaky boat motor.

What I do know, is that as much as Captain Bill was hated for the three hours we putted around that lake and as much as he put a damper on the festivities and as much as my friend's daughter would have liked to trade him out for Steamboat Willie, not a single person dove off the Pontoon boat that day.

And, that may have been the difference between one of us living to see another.

One of us living to see another.

"

Sweetie, I don't believe in love at first sight — love is
too complicated a thing to be felt in a single, initial
glance. But, when you do see him for the first time,
you should wonder where he's been. He should look
strangely familiar to you. It should feel as if, some-
time, in a past life, the two of you got separated in
a great crowd and much much later on, there is this
sudden break in the masses — the two of you look
up to see the other looking back, both wondering
where the other ran off to. This is how it should
feel, less like love and more like a beautiful falling
back into step.

"

A beautiful falling back into step.

We step into an elevator
and press five.
It takes us up to Matt and Mak's:
a flat with a wrap-around porch
so vast they'd swoon over it
down here in Tennessee.

On this wrap-around porch there are people:
pretty people,
people in love,
people finding love,
people in-between love.
I'm the wallflower clinging to the balcony
swallowing the cityscape,
swallowing the Brooklyn Bridge,
swallowing the Hudson,
swallowing the starry night burning blue,
swallowing glimpses of you —

dancing,
smiling,
laughing.

Your heart is bursting
like the fireworks
you keep pointing to
across the water
turning to spiders in the sky.

Spiders in the sky.

Raising hell,
like lightning in a night sky.

Raising hell,
like a bad dress and a white lie.

Raising hell,
like a rich kid in a necktie.

Raising hell,
like two gals, one guy.

Raising hell,
like Lucifer getting claustrophobic.

Raising hell,
like 1980s Jane Fonda, tights, aerobics.

1980s Jane Fonda, tights, aerobics.

I woke to golden lines in my eyes,
golden lines in my ears,
golden lines

slithering

across my white linens

like snakes

the sun had whispered
through my bedroom blinds

reminding me to write these lines,
reminding me to lace up my red wings
and grab a spade,
reminding me that Hemingway
is dead on the horizon.

Hemingway is dead on the horizon.

I'm your *Southern Indiana kid*, boy.
I'm your *reading candlelight*, boy.
I'm your *barefoot chasing fireflies*, boy.
I'm your *lacing up the red wings*, boy.
I'm your *gunning for pipe dreams*, boy.
I'm your *hunting down Hemingway*, boy.
I'm your *raising hell in Minsk, Belarus,* boy.
I'm your *getting read in seventy countries*, boy.
I'm your *can't hold down a woman*, boy.
I'm your *loyal only to the muse in my ear*, boy.

Loyal only to the muse in my ear, boy.

I'll be
your brown eyes
when you're tired of your green.

I'll be
your "come back to bed"
when you don't want to leave.

I'll be
your "sushi?" or "mexican?"
when you need choices.

I'll be
your hands on your tits,
hands on your hips,
hands on your ass,
hands between your legs,
when you need out of your mind.

I'll be
your home on the road
when you're gone chasing dreams.

I'll be
this summer's fling
next summer's fling

and every summer's fling
you give me after that.

Every summer's fling you give me after that.

I'm romantic about vinyl, red wings, cigarettes
and Duke's elbow-worn bar-top.

I'm romantic about pretty strangers, fire-escapes,
front porches, my grandfather's callused hands
and the stories he weaves with them.

I'm romantic about the morning's first cup of coffee.

I'm romantic about what Johnny said about June
when asked what his idea of paradise was...

"This morning, with her, having coffee."

I'm romantic about books.
I'm romantic about their spines.
I'm romantic about the pages these spines

protect
and keep neat
and keep straight
and keep good.

I'm romantic about Southern Indiana.
I'm romantic about basketball.
I'm romantic about bare feet on green grass.
I'm romantic about the fireflies that kept me

and my brothers from stubbing our naked toes
on all those no-moon nights.

I'm romantic about my brothers.
I'm romantic about bourbon.
I'm romantic about Four Roses.
I'm romantic about roses.

I'm romantic about the roses
I burned into my arm
to remind myself to keep being romantic
after a time when romance tasted
like a mouthful of blackwidows.

I'm romantic about summers in Chicago.
I'm romantic about winters in Colorado.
I'm romantic about autumns in Tennessee.
I'm romantic about the planes that take me
to these places with the shifting of the seasons.

And, I'm romantic about these same planes,
taking me home.

Planes, taking me home.

Near the edges of her eyes,
where the corneas kiss the sea of white,
there is a sunset yellow that exists there,
as if after creating them

God uncapped his highlighter
and circled his work,
making certain the world
would not skim past
what he had written.

What he had written.

Rachel,
there is nothing sensible
about love.

You do know that,
don't you?

You feel crazy
because you are crazy.

You've lost all your sense.
Every bit of it
has taken up residence
in the story left unwritten
between the two of you.

Remove the judgment,
stop posing questions
to your friends.

Your mother is a nightmare,
stop looking to her.

Just keep tearing through the pages,
dog-earing the splendid days,
underling the moments
you never want to forget.

However,
to answer your question,
I'm not certain yet how any of it will end.
I'm still writing the fucking book.

But,
I promise:
it won't be cancer.

But, I promise: it won't be cancer.

Catherine
smokes cigarettes
like she's late
for lunch
with Jesus Christ.

Catherine
cakes on that
cheap perfume
like she's
scared to death
he'll wonder
how she arrived
so soon.

Catherine,
killing time,
whispers
something pretty
in another lover's ear
that smells
of dead daisies
in an ashtray.

Dead daisies in an ashtray.

You're in our room asking for more,

I walk out.

I walk back in.

You're still in our room,
asking for more.

We smoke cigarettes

and we lie naked

and we lie to one another
about it still being our room.

We lie to one another about it still being our room.

Two, maybe three years back,
I'm home
because something is dying
inside of me
and I need my momma.

God
I need my momma.

And I say nothing
because boys like me
don't talk to their mommas
when they're dying,
scared
they're gonna break
their momma's hearts.

But mommas have a way
of smelling this dying,
of knowing this dying,
of feeling this dying,
having felt their boys' heartbeats
inside of them
so close to their hearts,
once upon a time.

And she sees me
passing through the living room
and she walks up to me
and she throws her arms around me
and she looks up at me
and she says:

"You know,
I don't tell you enough
how beautiful you are..."

And then she presses her face
in my chest
and she squeezes tight,
tighter,
tighter even,
and then she releases me
and returns to her day,

unaware she had saved my life.

Unaware she had saved my life.

It's the obvious that makes a woman beautiful.
It's the less obvious, too.
It's her living for a cause.
It's her hips mauled by tiger claws.
It's her becoming too much woman, too quickly.
It's her feeling like your mother when you turn sickly.
It's coffee with her.
It's wine with her.
It's vinyl with her.
It's silence with her.

It's her running her fingers through the hair you don't
have anymore.

It's Disneyland in a grocery store.
It's Heaven between her thighs.
It's the angels that share her breath.
It's the angels that take yours.
It's tomorrow growing inside.
It's her putting up her life for it.
It's as Bukowski writes...

"It's how well she walks through the fire..."

It's how well she walks through the fire.

It was
last winter
when their love became
a California summer,

when their love ran dry,
when their hatred became kindling
that turned their hearts to forest fires,
when their conversation became
a game of Russian roulette —

click,
click,
click,
click,
click,
bang,

when their words became daggers,
when their sex became life rafts,
when their kindness became conditional,
when their car rides became purgatories,
when their dinners became an orchestra

of forks and knives

clawing at porcelain plates,

when they became two devils
playing violins
drowning in the silence,

Rocks, heavy, in their pockets.

Rocks, heavy, in their pockets.

I'm writing at some haunt in East Nashville,
burying my nose in Didion,
nipping away at my iced coffee
in-between turned pages.

To my right sits a good-looking redhead
drowning in an oversized white dress shirt
that glows whiter against her off-white skin.

She's sporting a pair of clunky Skechers
that sit like cinder blocks beneath her long legs
that stretch for miles.

After bites of her Everything Bagel,
she brushes the bellies of her hands together,
decrumbing them,
like she's ridding herself of something troublesome
that has burdened her for far too long.

She's trying to read.
She can't read.
She's distracted,
stealing glances at her phone,
warring back a smile,
fighting desperately not to fall in love
too quickly
with the person on the other line.

I reach for a pad of paper.
She's material.
It's all material.
The good.
The bad.
The ugly.
The devils.
The demons.
The Dandelion wine.
The red-headed strangers,
sitting pretty as angels in coffee shops,
eating Everything Bagels
and falling in love
with people in places they'd rather be.

Falling in love with people in places they'd rather be.

A coffee shop on a Sunday is a curious place to be. Most especially if you're alone. It's curious because it means that on a day when society and neighbors and biblical texts and even employers grant you permission to take rest, you're doing nothing of the sort.

One might arrive at a coffee shop on a Sunday with every good intention of not doing something ambitious and one always finds oneself not abiding by this good intention; for coffee shops are perfectly fine places to dream and create and write and wonder what life could be.

If I'm telling truths, I began this piece not knowing where exactly I was writing to. I still don't know for certain. But, as I flick sentences from my fingers like the wet color from an abstract painter's brush, this piece is beginning to take form. Or, at least it soon will. Writing is like painting in this way. When I can't write, I take the unspoken advice of the painter and I put ink to paper.

Five, six, seven evenings ago, I was drinking wine and drawing and painting with my girl, who is quite possibly the most creative individual I know, the type of creative individual that leaves a creative individual like myself feeling a bit insecure. And, as she stood in front of her canvas hovering her dry brush above a palette full of color, she said so beautifully...

"I know it sounds cliche but the hardest thing about painting is placing your brush on the canvas."

I stopped drawing what I was drawing — a horse intended to be a horse that, unfortunately, took the shape of a giraffe — and I made a mental note to take what she had said and put it in some filing cabinet in my mind to pull from and write about later on. This is later on. So, when you can't write, you first do as the painter does and you do the hardest thing there is: you put pen to paper. But, after this, you must look up and you must look around.

Right now, sitting in this coffee shop, looking up and looking around, this is what I see:

I see nobody reading Jane Austen. I do, however, see an African American gentleman sporting a crimson button-down and a pair of leather loafers that have the tired look of having been worn a long time. He's staring very seriously at his laptop, his eyebrows bunching up the skin between them like the folds in a heavy curtain. Every now and again he will pound away like an angry pianist at the iPad lying beside his laptop. It appears that he's doing math. It appears that he works in finance. It appears he's counting money. It appears he's calculating how to make more money. He looks the part. He looks like a rich man. But, that fold of skin between his eyebrows gives away a truth (and since we are telling truths): he doesn't feel he is rich enough.

Sitting to his left (and my right) is a fair-skinned African American woman.

(Looking at that line, I can't decide if I should more readily reach for "light-skinned" versus "fair-skinned" while "fair-skinned" reads a bit prettier than "light-skinned," at least on the page, it gives this notion that to be light of complexion is "fair" and to be dark of complexion is "unfair" — an essay for another day, perhaps.)

She has more hair than I've ever seen atop someone's head, hair that takes off, willy nilly, like the falling limbs and leaves of a Willow Tree. She leaves it untethered while she reads a gorgeous book the color of a Macaw and jots down thoughts in a journal the color of a Magpie.

Once she feels she has emptied the well, she ties the willow up and into something tight and once secure, she begins knitting. She seems to be the only person in the coffee shop not dead set on taking over the world.

If the financier to her right (my left) were to watch her exist for but a few moments, he'd discover something the numbers weren't showing him: that being rich is about having enough money to buy experiences while having a bit leftover to stow away so that you can enjoy these experiences without the lingering concern that you won't be able to pay the rent.

As I watch these two, I realize that I'm the space between

them. I'm a lightning bug throwing himself back and forth against the invisible walls of the jar that are their shoulders.

Some days, I want the whole world or nothing at all. I want to dance in and out of writing genres with the ease and grace and ferocity of some jaguar that can't be kept and I want to be paid handsomely for this dancing and I want to take my handsome purse and spend it on fast cars and fine drink and suits that give the appearance that I am somebody. I am somebody. Pray tell me I'm somebody?

Other days, I want to climb into my '89 Range Rover with its peeling paint and chirps and hums and violent squeaks that could kill a symphony. I want to watch June leap into the backseat and be surprised by how, with each passing day, she seems to be growing more and more athletic. I want to grab a cup of coffee, enough to get me 100 miles down the road and perhaps 100 miles more. And, I want to leave my ambitions behind me.

While there is so much room for dreaming inside these coffee shops. I do wonder, from time to time, if these high ceilings leave any room for living; knitting.

Living; knitting.

We're seated at a small,
rectangular table,
just big enough to house
a couple of drinks
and a pair of elbows.

Right in front of us is a window
that opens up to a busy street
where people and cars can be seen
racing here and racing there.

If you sit back far enough,
the window makes a frame
and after a couple of drinks,
it feels as if you're watching a living,
breathing painting inside this frame;
a living breathing painting
that can't seem to make up its mind
what it wants to be.

What it wants to be.

"

You spend the first two decades of your life grab-assing
with your peers behind a proverbial pace car — getting
drunk in river camps, falling in love, falling out of love,
falling on your face, crying about it, laughing about it,
learning and unlearning and then learning again until,
suddenly, the pace car takes an exit, the motors rev and
then you're all off to the races — and in the matter of
two, maybe three years, you look up to see a few of your
ex-peers have been hiding some serious horsepower
underneath their hoods; enough horsepower to send
fissures down into hell.

"

Send fissures down into hell.

She did it
for the first time
in her bedroom
on the armrest
of her favorite chair.

She was sitting there
and the sitting began
feeling good
and she sat
a bit harder,
her thighs
hugging it tighter,
a good friend
she didn't know existed,
a good friend
taking her higher.

One evening,
her mother
caught her.

She stormed in
and struck her
cursing the soul
of her teary-eyed daughter

After this,
much older,
sex is something to be hidden,
sex is something to be ashamed of,
sex is something she's not worthy of,
sex is something devils do behind closed doors
sex is something angels condemn high above,

on their thrones,
on their chairs,

avoiding the lure
of their arm rests
like Satan's tongue.

Satan's tongue.

"

When you're a man or a woman in your early twenties you're in this very strange place with love where you're not ready to commit to what it takes to enjoy it, not fully, but you still long to feel it and you still desperately want the possibility to be there, with someone, if one day you wake up and decide that it's something you're ready to pursue. It's this strange contrast between wanting to remain "free" while at the same time wanting to be "wanted" whilst enjoying this freedom. And, so, like a serial killer, you take pretty women's hearts and you pack them full of ice and you place them in a safe and then you live wildly with the comfort of knowing someone, somewhere, is going to love you in those moments when you can't love yourself or in those moments where you've run out of distractions from the stark realization that you don't love yourself. In these moments, you write her and you tell her just how much you'd like to see her and it's not her you're wanting to see but instead the way she sees you, the way she looks at you. Then, you ice her, once again. Eventually, she cracks the code to this safe, thaws out her heart and she takes it back without you knowing, and one night you find yourself piss drunk in Chicago, Illinois, writing her because things with the woman that isn't her aren't going as planned and she doesn't write back. The safe is empty. The safe is empty. The safe is empty. Then, she does the cruelest trick our past lovers ever play on us. She does not call. She does not write. She waits for your head to hit your pillow and for your dreams to become your reality and it's there where she visits you, loves you, fucks you, walks hand-in-hand with you, tells you it's going to be alright. But, it's just a dream.

"

But, it's just a dream.

I'm romantic about the way she looks at me
when I get off of the plane,
her pulling up to the BNA as pretty as an afternoon daydream,
her brown hair a mess above her head,
her smile killing me,
killing me,
killing me,
then bringing me back to life,
holding me,
holding me tight,
like I could float away again.

I could float away again.

The sky is falling
(apart) one tear at a time.

Crying on my lashes.
Crying on my cheeks.
Crying on my lips.
Crying on my beat-to-hell Sauconys.
Crying on my beat-to-hell Range.
Crying on its windows.

Its old windshield wipers
licking away the crying,
crying,
crying.

Each sweep
a fool's errand,
licking away the crying;
a pair of wicker brooms
shooing away the tide,
licking away the crying,
crying,
crying.

Crying,
the whole drive
home.

Crying, the whole drive home.

God is on the corner of Gallatin and Eastland Avenue
holding a grocery bag,
heaping with twenty-five pounds of ribeyes
he lifted from the Kroger behind him.

He's watching the streetlight to the left of him,
waiting for it to turn from green to red,
waiting for the cars to stop racing by.

He grows impatient and lifts up a black hand
and the light turns and the cars gunning down Gallatin
come to a screeching halt.

He saunters across the street to a woman in a wheelchair
wearing a pair of sweatpants the sun has turned patina,
smoking a chewed up cigarette.

She grins, toothless.

He grins back a smile as white as Columbian Cocaine.

He drops three ribeyes, neatly packaged, right there in her lap.
He keeps walking as she turns them over in her hand
like they're gold, like they're the flesh of Christ.

And, I'm watching all of this from a rumbling 89' Range
as patinaed as this woman's sweats,
wondering how she's going to grill them.

At this thought, God whips around with squinting eyes
he turns on me, telling me behind closed lips
to go buy her a charcoal grill.

Go buy her a charcoal grill.

Evening,
Chicago.

Reminiscing,
months ago,
nearly a year ago,
forever ago.

Praying,
the falling snow
will delay her flight
home.

Leaning,
her into him,
her hair falling.

Snaking,
its way around
copper buttons.

Looking,
at the clock
on the wall.

Pleading,
the time will move slower.

Dwindling,
eight hours
and then seven hours
and then five
and then...

Is this what we signed up for,
baby?

Honking,
outside a taxi waits.

Growing,
ever impatient
as she gathers her things
like firewood.

Kissing,
one last time
until the next time
it's time to have
the time of their lives.

Watering,
her eyes
like snow turned
warm.

Lying,
saying it's just the cold.

Stepping,
inside.

Slamming,
the door.

Existing,
now worlds away.

Existing, now worlds away.

I looked at her
in much the same way
a woman in the twilight of her years
looks back on a faded photograph
of her younger self

enamored,
enthralled,
enchanted

while at the same time
holding back the urge
to reach out my hands,
taking hold of her brilliant face,
shaking her,
cursing her,
for not knowing
she has the entire fucking world
sitting pretty in her lap,
and the eyes
and the lips
and the legs
and the brains
to make the men in it
dance to any tune of her choosing.

Dance, to any tune of her choosing.

I'm walking home at 11 p.m. on a Friday night,
sipping a bottle of Gatorade
and carrying a bag full of snacks
I picked up from the gas station
down the road from my home.

Across the street an angry-looking white woman
is standing on her patio with her arms crossed.

She's my neighbor but she doesn't know it.

I'm brown but the no-moon night paints me black.
She yells across the street at me
and I turn to her and I smile at her
and all she can see are my white teeth.

She announces to me
that several cars in the neighborhood
have been broken into.

I say nothing.
She asks me if I know anything about it.
I say no.
She asks me where I live.
I say in the neighborhood.
She asks me where in the neighborhood.
I say down the street.

She shakes her head.
She tells me she has a policeman patrolling.
She turns and she walks inside.

If I didn't have so much to lose,
I would have gone into her home after her
and I would have grabbed her by her hair
and I would have dragged her down
Cleveland Street
letting the asphalt turn her skin
the color she so deeply hates
and I would drag her through
my home
up to the deck that sits above it,
and I'd point from my rooftop to her home
and then I'd toss her over the edge
where her blood would lacquer my driveway
like the cherry red paint on all those
1989 Jaguar XJS V12s
my Japanese grandmother adored
but could never afford.

Instead,
I just smiled at her,
sipping my Gatorade,
swinging my grocery bag of snacks,
continuing my walk home,
even though I no longer had the
stomach to eat them.

The stomach to eat them.

Her panties,
thin,
like
dental floss.

Wet,
as if
they spent
the afternoon
flossing
the teeth
of the tiger
on my arm.

Warm,
as if
he liked
the taste,
and swallowed them
whole.

Now,
they're
discarded,
forgotten,
abandoned,
an after-thought,

like his last meal.

An after-thought, like his last meal.

Taylor and I, we're eating oysters at a small oyster stand in a massive hotel with high ceilings. The company that owns the oyster stand is called Murder Bay.

I tell the owner I dig the aesthetic. Taylor tells the owner his logo looks vaguely similar to a vagina. It does. Things get awkward after this. I go sit down and drink my wine and think about how much better vaginas taste than oysters.

We leave the massive hotel and its high ceilings and go to another massive hotel with high ceilings.

It's called The Dream Hotel. There's an open bar. Taylor and I and another friend named Kirsten begin to drink and we don't stop.

Another friend joins us. He just got a new job. It's not as cool as his old job. But, less heavy. At his old job, he would jump on a plane and transport human hearts from one state to another when someone died so someone else could live.

That's the prettiest line in this piece. That's the prettiest line in this book.

This friend doesn't stop drinking, either.

I see two white roses in a pretty blue vase next to me. I take them and a bottle of champagne. I lose one of them to a pretty face. I lose the other one on my doorstep only to find it the next morning. It's a bit tattered and dirty but still lovely despite its tattered and dirtiness.

It reminds me of this morning's hangover.

It reminds me of this morning's hangover.

Standing at the punch bowl,

swallowing punch,
staring at a sea of strangers,
hunting for material,
hunting for Moby Dick,
writing lines in-between pulls of punch,
writing lines in-between pulls of blood,
all the while not pulling punches:
even though your mother is reading,
even though your friends are reading,
even though your girl is reading,
even though your ex-girl is reading.

Later on,
sitting at the typewriter,
swallowing blood.

Sitting at the typewriter, swallowing blood.

"

Fuck. You don't see it, do you? You're dying. You've been dying. You started dying the moment you entered your twenties and you were forced to make this transition from you expecting something off the world to the world expecting something off you. Year after year after year you're murdering yourself. Twenty-three. Twenty-four. Twenty-five. Twenty-six. The years of your youth are sweeping by like the lights of the towns in the windows of the passing train car. You are the passing train car. As I write this now I can see my years, passing and then dead, rotting, stinking to heaven, tickling the nose of Jesus Christ, making him nervous. You, myself, all of us are killing off ourselves for something. And, you not choosing something to murder these years away for, to sacrifice your youth for, doesn't make you immune to this fact. It just means you're killing off your years for indecision, inaction.

"

Indecision, inaction.

Standing in the doorway of her room
like a ghost with boots
in two worlds.

I look at her lying in bed
and then out the window
at the rain
and then back at her,
again.

"You're crazy,"

she says.

"Get back in bed."

Get back in bed.

For a while, it was a dream. It's still a dream when I look back before the call she received the following Spring.

We moved into a flat in Wicker, a stone's throw away from Lucky's. She decorated the whole goddamn place in plants. She had the greenest of thumbs. We talked about kids but we decided we'd hold off until I was made executive at my agency and she could finish her schooling. She was studying to become a psychologist.

We were living a dream until she got a call about her headaches. We were drinking coffee right beside our bay window where she kept dozens and dozens of succulents in these tiny hand-made pieces of pottery she so very much adored.

Ironically, on this particular day, her head wasn't bothering her one bit. We were sipping and going from silence to laughing and back again. I think that's what love is, drinking coffee and laughing and falling hard in the silence that comes after laughing. And, in one of these silences, the phone rang and she answered and the voice on the other end of the line made her face change and I remember her eyes were just as pretty as they've ever been as our dream was cut short.

She passed three months later.

When the love of your life makes her French Exit, what hurts the most is the silence. It's a bit absurd how horrible silence is when she's not in the same room to share it.

And, once you get past the silence, there is a long while where seeing and experiencing all the pretty little things that made her wildly happy is the closest you come to hell on earth.

Eventually, when the loneliness becomes too much, you find yourself at one of those bars the two of you would frequent, now alone, looking for a body to keep you warm and to numb the ache.

And, if you're lucky, you find one.

That night, it's a sanctuary. But, when you wake up the next morning and she's lying there next to you, her hair won't be the right color and her skin won't be the right shade and her eyes won't be the same blue and she'll look different sleeping there, twisted in the sheets.

I think that's half of falling out of love with — or at the very least moving past — someone you've lost, learning to fall out of love with the shape they embodied as they existed in the world.

It's been a good while and I'm still falling out of love with the shape of you.

Falling out of love with the shape of you.

"

In Plato's Symposium, he writes that early humans were androgynous, possessing two sets of everything: arms, legs, hands, feet, faces, eyes, etc, etc, etc. These beings were strong and fast, traveling around the world at alarming speeds by cartwheeling. This frightened the Gods. So much so that Zeus cut them in half. For the remainder of their days, each half longed for the other and so they would press their faces together and they'd throw their arms and their legs around one another — weaving, tangling, intertwining — desperately trying to get closer, to grow together again.

"

To grow together again.

Her hips
pressed
against mine,
velcroed,
unmoving.

Her ass
buried
in my lap,
buckled,
in its seat.

Her back
arched,
her spine,
a bucket slide

I want to come
down.

I want to come down.

Her mouth is open
like the oxygen in my room
has turned to cherries

and her lips are pursed
as if she's doing away
with their pits

and her eyes are closed
as if they're too good
to be true

and her fingers are caressing
my face
and my ears
and my neck
and my shoulders
and my arms
as if my skin has turned to
braille.

My skin has turned to braille.

We're gunning
for the BNA
so she can catch a flight
out to LA
to paint the cover
of another magazine.

At the light,
she takes a photograph
of her and I
and she sends it my way
before she's up in the sky.

And it's the first time
I see her and I existing
in the same frame.

Before this,
falling for her
was photographs of her
and only her
taken through my eyes.

Taken through my eyes.

She pulls up in a black Audi the size of a Hummer and steps out in a pair of faded pink Adidas, white-washed jeans three sizes too big, and a skin-tight tank top whiter than her.

I'm looking at her from a chair on the patio, my legs crossed, mind soft off two shots of whiskey I took to drench the butterflies in kerosene; the butterflies I knew her face would flutter in me.

My first impression of her face is her jawline. I want to slice my lips open on its edges and have her kiss them clean. Then it's her eyes which walk this beautiful line between brown and green.

And, finally, it's her hair which is as thick and as dark as my momma's, thick enough to rip hair ties in two, thick enough to save a falling man, thick enough to saw down the Redwoods she says she wants to cling to when the spotlight burns too hot. The rest of the night I can't keep my hands out of this thick, dark hair. I'm a child lost in the woods.

I stand and I walk her way and I throw my arms around her and her small frame sinks beneath the depths of my denim jacket. It feels like we've embraced before.

I get in. We ride to a haunt up the road. Her Audi is so heavy I can almost feel the pavement cracking beneath us. She talks nothing like she texts.

The voice my mind's lips have been reading her in for the past few days didn't have enough twang, enough honey. I want to drown in the sound of her.

Inside, the room is dark and it is loud and then it is less so as people drunk and people less drunk break their necks at the recognition of her, at the sight of her. She's Tennessee's Jesus Christ.

I'm walking several paces behind her and like the wallflower I am, I'm trying desperately to keep my six-foot frame out of the giant shadow she casts.

We sit in a corner in the courtyard, my head buzzing from the madness. Her, unfazed. She looks up at me with those brownish-green eyes that can't seem to make up their mind and she asks, "What do you drink?"

What do you drink?

— Monday,

I spent the morning giving you head
in a bed so messy
its linens looked like it had
gobbled up an F5 Tornado

the night before,
your dreams sprouted shark teeth
and you went running in the night,

stopping only when the Tennessee sun
stuck her tongue through the blinds,
licking the sleep from our faces,

forcing open my eyes
towards your dark hair
spilling down your back
and onto the covers
like the shadow of a shade tree.

Like the shadow of a shade tree.

I found God playing a piano in Louisville
and I almost took a job selling drugs in Austin
and I saw angels collect around my pen in Nashville
and I chased Hemingway in Chicago
and I got paid to be a poor man's Ogilvy in Minsk
and I found love in Denver

(but the love was skinny
and my feet grew cold)

and so I trekked back down south,
my red wings as my saddle,
where I'm gonna live out the rest of my days
a stone's throw from the Cumberland
and take a big jet plane to New York
when the ink runs dry.

When the ink runs dry.

I just try and admit
that I'm impure,
that I'm unsure,
that I'm insecure.

I don't flex no more —
because there's strength in admitting I'm sore;
and there's calm in avoiding a war,
and there's content in not wanting more,
and there's confidence in not keeping score.

I like to think I'm winning
but I ashed the cigar-chomping
and I silenced the chest-thumping
and I stopped the dick-swinging
and I broke the high-handing,
realizing:

boasting about the bankroll in my britches
and the invisible bitches in my bed
wouldn't quiet the demons in my head.

So I stopped

writing that my face is pretty
because it was a disguise for my soul being shitty
and because you've got ears

that can hear lies
and you've got eyes
that can make up their own mind
and because,
let's face it,
a good-looking stare
ain't that hard to find in an era
with good lighting
and body sculpting
and magic filters that can turn somebody's bad day
or somebody's sad day
or somebody's worst day
or somebody's last day

into Christmas day.

Into Christmas Day.

Drunk.
Walking home.
11 p.m.
A Friday night.
Bag full of snacks
and Gatorade
to shoo away
tomorrow's hangover.
White neighbor,
arms crossed.
Yells,
across the street.
at my direction.
Me?
Me.

She says:
cars
have been
broken into.
Hers
and
her neighbor's.

She asks:
you wouldn't
know anything

about that,
would you?
It's summer.
The Japanese,
the Syrian.
turn me brown
like I'm Hispanic,
like I'm half Black,
like I'm half of something.
I point up the road
to a home
on the corner,
bigger than hers,
nicer than hers,
with a roof deck
you could land
a helicopter on.
She says nothing.
Arms crossed.
I keep walking.
Drinking Gatorade
like I just left the EBA
in Southern Indiana,
swinging
my bag of groceries
like the beautiful mutt I am;

a fucking oxymoron.

A fucking oxymoron.

She's terribly particular
about everything in her home.

Everything has a place:
the rugs
and the couches
and the crystal water glasses
and the whiskey bottles
and the driftwood bar stools
and the blown-up
photograph of her mother
sitting pretty
smoking a cigarette.

Even the q-tips are exactly
where they're supposed to be,
a tiny bouquet of white roses
in a small jar.

Art,

until they're called upon
to sweep her ears.

To sweep her ears.

I meet this blond-haired blue-eyed girl
at a Chicago coffee shop
called Ipsento 606.

She's got a fat wedding ring
wrapped around her finger.

She asks me to go back to her flat,
two blocks up the road.

I agree.

We arrive and we walk up the stairs
to her studio.

We sit down
at a great big wooden table
and she tells me to teach her
how to write.

I do for an hour or so.

Then I leave.

Before I do she hands me $500,
cash.

She says she will be calling again.

I say thank you
and then I leave.

I walk up North Milwaukee Avenue,
something good-sounding
is blaring in my earbuds.

I think to myself:

at twenty-five I didn't think I'd be here,
wherever here is.

And, now, editing this at twenty-eight,
I thought I'd be further up the road
than I am

now.

I thought I'd be further up the road than I am now.

I

see
Hemingway,
running,
up ahead.

His shadow
fastening the sky
to the earth
like a

railroad nail.

Railroad nail.

Sitting in a dimly lit basement bar beneath a claustropho-
bic ceiling, the back of my chair is brushing against an
exposed brick wall. I'm watching women with unmasked
faces smiling smiles that could cause a 7-car pile up.
They're gliding around barstools as grinning boys jockey
for position.

The room's centerpiece is a gal with red hair. It's combed
ketchup. It's pooling blood. It's a crimson you'd never want
painted on your walls but a crimson you can't help but
reach out and —

A part of me wants her, a part of me doesn't because
everyone in the room wants her. She's with a handsome
mustachioed man wearing a faded blue bomber jacket
with the big yellow embroidered name of a sports team I
doubt he follows. Her black purse hangs from one of his
broad shoulders.

A part of her wants him, a part of her doesn't because
everyone in the room wants her. She leans into him. He
grabs her ass. She lets him, until a man that isn't him who
she's been locking eyes with all night looks her way. She
bats away her coat rack's hand. She wants to be wanted but
not mistaken for being taken.

After a while she makes her way over to me. She strikes up

a conversation. Uneasy, he waves her over. She doesn't go. His uneasiness subsides, some, seeing his faded blue jacket hanging from her shoulders like a pair of melted angel wings. He knows a man would never kiss a woman wearing another man's jacket.

She reaches out her hand. I shake it. She says her name. I don't remember it. She asks me what I do. I lie because if I were to tell the truth it would have sounded more like a lie. Eventually, she tells me she's in fashion. It's here where I understand. She's shopping.

Men for her go in and out of style like the seasons and that jacket on her shoulders is getting too heavy and too warm with Spring just around the corner.

Upon this realization I'm a house cat losing interest. I look away, across the bar at a stage where a big-bearded man who looks like Chris Stapleton is singing Chris Stapelton. He is good. She notices.

She takes her angel wings to the stage to steal a closer look, her hair a strawberry wine spilling down her back like Lucifer, bleeding out.

Lucifer, bleeding out.

Hell emptied
this afternoon,
and its citizens
have taken up residence
in my head.

In my head.

"

It's not about changing how you feel nor apologizing for how you feel but instead understanding why you feel the way you feel. We are humans. Emotions are as much a part of us as our lungs and our hearts. So, to change how we feel or apologize for how we feel is changing or apologizing for the most human aspects of ourselves. I think the great divide we face is not in the emotions we feel but in not fully understanding why we are feeling them.

"

Feeling them.

She was beautiful.
Not beautiful by today's standards.
But, beautiful in that you could see the world
looking back at her in the future,
countless decades from now
and being in awe.

Looking at her was looking at living,
breathing vintage *Vogue*
that you knew by 3021
would read like poetry

— the girls would be pasting centerfolds
of her to their bathroom mirrors,
the boys would be masturbating to her
high above The Earth in their spaceships
and while long dead,
she'd finally get the attention
her beauty deserved.

She was a pending nostalgia.

She was a pending nostalgia.

She turns her head to the side,
flashing me a jawline.

Sharp enough
to chap my lips,

sharp enough
to slit my tongue,

sharp enough
to behead a monarch,

sharp enough
to kill a guillotine,

sharp enough
to turn Keira Knightley green.

To turn Keira Knightley green.

These pretty faced Instagram influencers
would lop off their heads
and give themselves head
if reattaching them
wouldn't leave behind scars.

So instead,
they change their profile pictures
like they got a dozen faces
they can't stand to look at for too long.

For too long.

Hate you, darling?
I don't hate you, darling.
I couldn't dare hate you, darling.
I hate that we came so close, darling.
I hate what we could have been, darling.
I hate what once was once upon a time, darling.
I hate that we're just a couple of strangers now, darling.
I hate that we're supposed to exist like the other doesn't, darling.

Doesn't, darling.

"

Every man has a small dick he's hiding. It's just not always a small dick. It might be his starving wallet. It might be his eroding hairline. It might be his right boot sticking out of the closet, the rest of him buried inside. It might be the burning hands of an adult at a young age. It might be broken teeth, premature ejaculation, a fractured heart, his wife on another man's arm, alcoholism, a Klonopin addiction, a disease that we can't see. And none of this matters unless you're going for empathy. If it's empathy you're after, it's worthwhile to remember that the mother fucker who just cut you off in traffic, his third finger pressed against the windshield like a Robin flying in the wrong place at the wrong time, has demons howling in his ear that you can't hear. And this is no excuse for bad behavior, but it is an excuse to attempt to understand.

"

Attempt to understand.

"

The energy we illuminate is a direct reflection of
our internal state. When we are judgmental, we are
judgmental within. When we are combative, we are
combative within. When we are angry, we are angry
within. When we are defensive, we are defensive
within. When we are anxious, we are anxious within.

In this way, our external energy and actions can act
as a second set of eyes that we can look through to
look within ourselves, allowing for a deeper aware-
ness of "self." When staring at yourself through
this second set of eyes, it's worthwhile not to do so
from a perspective of judgment because when we
are judgmental, we are judgmental within. Instead,
we should seek to look at ourselves and our actions
through a lens of curiosity. This begins by reframing
our thoughts and questions. The question is not:
"Why have I been an asshole lately?" The question
is: "I've been quick to temper lately. That's inter-
esting. I wonder why?" The phrase "That's inter-
esting..." invites further exploration without the
pressure of labeling our states and our moods and
our actions and our energies as being something
fundamentally bad or good.

This same outward set of eyes can be helpful in creating grace for not just ourselves but our friends, our family and strangers-in-passing. It keeps us from "reacting" to the states of those around us and makes room for "responding" with grace. Imagine how the dialogue would change between yourself and your humans if the question changed, if the question were no longer: "Why are you so defensive?" And, instead, if it became: "Are you hurting? Talk to me." This allows the individual on the receiving end of the question to feel seen and cared for and acknowledged, rather than attacked. It's a gentle reach within a person, rather than a sharp prick outside of them.

Perhaps, creating a better world, a world where it is easier to exist, begins not just with ourselves but within ourselves. By tending to ourselves internally, we illuminate a well-tended soul externally. From here, we can become a light in the rooms we enter and perhaps, something warm and bright and luminescent for those who need someone to light their way with grace, as they go about their own tending.

"

As they go about their own tending.

In Heaven,
there is
a vast
library of vinyl.

Records are flying off
the shelves,
left
and then right

carried by angels.

Everyone
is
fucking
everyone

to Winehouse
to Bon Iver
to Cigarettes After Sex
to Frank Ocean
to Kacey Musgraves

and,
not a damn person
is using protection
because

you can't catch the clap
in Heaven.

You can't catch the clap in heaven.

"

There's a lot of good shit you miss in porn; like pulling out but not being able to pull away from her pursed lips, dripping wet like a paint brush on her naked abdomen; after this, grabbing a towel to sponge up the paint because it isn't the kind of paint a woman wants to wear, at least not for too long, at least not once the moment has passed; then, discovering a good amount of paint has made its way down and into her belly button, where your could-be-children are having a good, warm bath.

You attempt to use the towel to sop up the paint from this reservoir only to find the towel is much too thick around your fingertip and her belly button is much too small, so you then have to use your finger, your bare finger, like your idiot adolescent self finger painting a turkey on a paper plate, you're being careful and gentle and thoughtful, recognizing that nobody in the history of humankind has ever enjoyed having a finger jammed in their belly button; finally, wondering if she could just get it out herself, then realizing she'd have cum caked in the underbellies of her acrylics.

And I'm not sure where I was going with any of that but someone needs to unpack the cum-in-the-belly-button fiasco that's currently plaguing America.

"

Plaguing America.

"

Your twenties are a glorious cluster-fuck. They're spent working jobs you hate for people you hate. They're spent trying not to hate yourself. They're spent hating yourself anyway. They're spent making more dough than you ever have before yet still feeling a little bit broke. They're spent comparing and contrasting everything you have to everything everyone else has. They're spent losing your best friends to pretty women. They're spent winning and failing, loving and failing, fucking and failing. They're spent hoping, pleading, begging, praying to a God you're not sure you believe in anymore, that there will be less cluster-fucks in your thirties. And, perhaps, a hell of a lot more glory.

"

Perhaps, a hell of a lot more glory.

You strip naked
and you shave the crook
of your neck
and the bits between your legs
and even the tiny whiskers that sprout
from the tops of your feet.

You do this so when
the lightning strikes
and you don't catch it
but it catches you,
the burning hair on your smoldering body
isn't the last thing you
have to smell before you die.

You'll then wait for a storm,
a good one,
one that sends
bright yellow electric dragons
roaring and fucking and parading
behind the clouds.

You'll hear them
like banshees in the distance
from your bedroom window.

You'll grab a sturdy bottle
and sprint out to the woods

and find a tree that towers above the rest.

You'll hold up your bottle
and lightning will come
surging down,
lurching,
falling,
striking
its way with vengeance
into the top of that great tall tree
and in the blink of an eye,
it will race to the bottom
to meet you where you're standing,
naked,
sacrificing everything you love,
even your own life,
for the chance to capture it,
in that outstretched hand of yours,
for just a moment.

And a few,
a select few of us
will get wildly lucky and escape with our lives,
lightning in hand
and our souls still intact.

And the rest of us will get mostly lucky,
dying

whilst trying to do the impossible.

Dying whilst trying to do the impossible.

"

If you're not careful, you subconsciously start
designing your life absent of the word "no," absent
of any sort of rejection. You "nerf" yourself in order
to save yourself from any pain, from any disappoint-
ment, from any loss, from any sadness, from any
feeling less than comfortable, in hopes to not ever
experience another day that feels like you're dying
— and with this savings, you cost yourself elation,
euphoria, pleasure. You cost yourself the cream that
floats to the top of life's milk like the clouds that sat
above Pompeii.

"

Pompeii.

When a part of his brain died, the man that stood taller than the towers that lined Chicago came crashing to the ground.

When I first saw him, he was seated hunched over in a wheelchair, clumsily forking spaghetti into his mouth with his left hand because his right hand no longer worked.

The room was dark, save for a tiny Christmas tree that cast shadows on the walls and ceiling like broken dreams.

He came to, just for a little while.

He saw me but he couldn't match a face with a name. I hugged him longer and harder than I ever have before and I kissed the top of his bald head, the hot water from my eyes painting trails on his skin.

Eventually, I found the courage to let go and he began to eat his spaghetti again with tears in his eyes that once looked like mine.

I'm not sure he remembered how they got there.

I didn't say anything, for a good while, letting the silence do what it does best, quiet the elephant in the room.

He killed the trumpeting beast, asking me if I thought he'd be worth a damn again.

And, that question broke my heart.

And, that question broke my heart.

My grandfather's hands are art.

Years of laboring and tinkering and working have
transformed them into something more than hands,
something like living breathing tools.

They're worn in like two Rawlings baseball gloves
that have seen a dozen seasons and they're protected
by callouses as thick as chainmail, so rough that with
enough rubbing he could turn a burlap bag into silk.

They're heavy too. "Dense" is how I would describe
them. They're not something you want to be hit with.

He told me a story once, reflecting on his tenure
in the Navy where he worked on a submarine for
months at a time, buried deep within the ocean.

Another sailor ran his mouth about something or
another, calling my grandfather's mother something
or another, and my grandfather swept around and hit
him in the side of the nose with the back of his hand.

The strike turned the sailor's schnoz into a bloody
gore that hung down his face like a dilapidated flag.

Apparently, they had to stitch him up from the base of the nostril to the inner corner of his eye to make him whole again.

My grandfather's hands have been guilty of spinning tall tales.

Guilty of spinning tall tales.

The taxi drops him off at a bar called The Bulla at 6:29 p.m.
on a Monday night because he's been drinking
and because he's got a date at 6:30 p.m.

He walks in by 6:31 p.m in a pair of green tapered cargo pants,
in an oversized button-down colored a faded maroon
you can only find in a thrift store.

Colors are clashing, fabrics are contrasting,
yet somehow he looks put together.

He walks up to the bar and he leans in
and he reaches his left arm around a brunette he met at a coffee shop
the afternoon before.

He asked if he could buy her next cup.
She said no.
Later, she came up to him, having changed her mind.
But, instead she wanted wine.

Now, here they are.
She's sipping something red like it's the blood of Jesus Christ
and his hands are hugging the copper mug of a Kentucky Mule
like it's the key to the pearly gates.
He finishes one.
He orders another.
He finishes one.
He orders another.

She keeps pace:
more red,
more red,
more red.

She's so good-looking he can't look at her directly.

She's a little under six feet.
She's got legs that run for miles,
legs that could squeeze a barstool in half,
an ass that would send men tumbling out
second and third-floor windows,
hair as thick as the evergreens
that sprout from the mountains of Utah.
And, worst yet, she dresses well.
My god, does she dress well.
They have good conversation and in this conversation
he catches her looking at him
like she's never sat across from a strange fellow like him.

Eventually, he asks her:

I'm not really your type, am I?

And she smiles
and she laughs
and she shakes her head
and part of her leans in
and part of him leans away
because he can't do long-distance,

again.

Long distance, again.

It's been painful to sit back
quietly watching you love her so intensely
and not watching this love be reciprocated.

At times,
it has felt not unlike watching
a heavy-weight boxer pummel
a steel beam.

He pounds
and he pounds
and he pounds
and the steel beam doesn't budge.

He goes to bed with bloody knuckles
and wakes up the next morning
and continues with the pounding.

Ever-bloody,
his knuckles become
and still the steel beam doesn't budge.

That's what it has felt like
watching you fight for her love

— like watching a heavyweight boxer
fight a steel beam.

And,
it's worst yet,
because

the boxer is my brother.

The boxer is my brother.

If I weren't a writer
I'd be a boxer,
a barista,
a formula one driver,
a dog walker,
a professional assassin,
a sushi chef,
a tattoo artist,
a shinto priest,
a prostitute,
a painter

or one of the folks who dye blue jeans blue.

One of those folks who dye blue jeans blue.

The man with a painter's soul
hanging drywall for a living
here on earth,

won't be hanging
drywall
in heaven.

Hanging drywall in heaven.

I think some women want
desperately to know that you can't go on
without them;

that you can't exist without them;

that after them you'll never be the same;

and I think this is where I've always run into trouble;

because even in the moments
I'm fucked beyond recollection
with a heavy heart
that feels like it could come crashing
through the floor;

I can write.

I can write.

Let me tell you,
all poets are whores.

They might not be whores
in the traditional sense.

But, every last one of them
are writing,
to varying degrees,
for the applause
of their readers.

Don't let them tell you any different.

I'll keep stripping
on this piece of paper
until you feel something,
until you validate me.

I'm not any different
from the whore you'd find
working the nightshift
at the corner store.

Corner store.

You stumble drunk through Five Points in East Nashville and eventually, a cherry red neon sign reading "Duke's" will catch your eye. Its glow draws you in with the same bewitching magic as the lure of an angler fish and before you know it, your feet are moving in the glow's direction.

On the other side of the glow, inside, it's dark and it's dingy and it's louder than you'd expect it to be. The bar top is as worn as a boxer's nose and just as crooked; decorated with nicks and bruises and scratches and dents from the countless drinks and heavy elbows and drunken ring-clad fists thrust upon its surface to emphasize a point that nobody will remember come morning.

You walk in there with $35 and you can leave not knowing your head from your ass. There is a deal at Duke's called "The Patriot." For $7 you get a tall pour of lager and a shot of Four Roses. You walk in with a bit of pocket change and a can-do attitude and you can leave a couple hours later with a belly full of beer and 5 shots of good clean bourbon sloshing around in your stomach.

If all this drinking leaves your stomach chirping, you can order one of their sandwiches. They have big sandwiches. Small sandwiches. Hot sandwiches. Cold sandwiches. Italian sandwiches. Vegetarian sandwiches. Spicy sandwiches.

They even have build-your-own sandwiches. In the midst of this building, my conversation with the bartender is always the same. He yanks out his order form, mashes his pen into his hand. I start gunning, listing off everything I want and he writes like hell to keep up. It's fucking poetry...

"... Honey Maple Turkey. Tavern Ham. Extra meat, please. Monterey Jack with the Jalapeno. Spinach. Tomato. Red Onion. Hot Giardiniera or however the fuck you say it. Pickles. Herbed Mayo. Olive Oil..."

I then sit down with my cold beer and Roses and look over my shoulder every so often waiting for that sandwich to come my way.

If I'm not eating alone, I cheers. If I'm eating alone, I cheers, and then I start writing something longhand.

Something longhand.

I'm getting older but my momma can still break my heart.
I'm getting older but I still make a skateboard out of the grocery cart.
I'm getting older but I still cry when I think about my parents dying.
I'm getting older but I still have trouble sleeping after a day of lying.
I'm getting older but I still remember my grandma's perfume.
I'm getting older but I'm still that little boy in the bathroom.
I'm getting older but I'm still a sucker for an anime and some pocky.
I'm getting older but I'm still

I'm getting older but I'm still

Growing up
is experiencing
the hell
of not having
something
you want more
than any other
something,

Growing up
is standing good
and standing tall,
despite
not having
this something.

Not having this something.

"

We can be great. Or, we can be something better
than great and that's good. Good to ourselves.
Good to others. Good to our family. Good to our
friends. Good to strangers. Good to the memories
of those that graced this planet before us. Good to
the possibilities of those still waiting to grace it. We
can be good. We can be good. We can be good.

"

We can be good.

God bless,
all those pretty white girls,
going to church on Sunday morning,
in their sun dresses,
cum still on their breath.

Lingering,
like garlic.

Lingering,
like lost religion.

Lingering,
ghosts in places
they cannot leave.

In places they cannot leave.

Just the other day I was sitting at my desk staring
out my window when a bird flew into it. It was
painted a pretty speckled brown and it had a cream
colored belly that resembled cashmere.

I went outside, hoping it would fly again, only to
find it wouldn't.

It was lying there, struggling to breathe, unable
to move, with each gasp losing a little bit more of
itself. It was hell to watch.

I went and grabbed a spade to end its misery and
when I returned, guillotine in hand, the grass where
it lay was still warm and it held the shape where it
once was

but it was gone.

But it was gone.

"

Live well and live fully, live leaving everything on
the line. Live for your craft and live with the under-
standing that you're sacrificing your life for your
craft. And, so live choosing a good one, live choos-
ing one worth dying for, live choosing one that will
leave the world a better place. And, in between
the living for this craft, live never passing up on an
opportunity to laugh with friends, love on friends,
cherish friends and drink with friends. And, in the
mornings that follow, when you must pay the tax on
this laughing and this loving and this cherishing and
this drinking, live nobly, taking the hangover on the
chin, smiling and bloody, spitting out teeth, spitting
out teeth, spitting out teeth. Live never losing those
rose-colored glasses stowed away in your back pock-
et. Live knowing that tomorrow will be better even
in those afternoons when you're existing in hell.
Live removing some weight from your shoulders,
realizing that at the end of the day, we're all just
stardust floating through the Milky Way and that
none of this matters and that's the very reason why
all of this matters... because we're stardust ambi-
tious enough to think we can leave our mark on a
galaxy that cares nothing about us and, that some-

how, we keep beating the odds, again and again and again. Live like this isn't forever. Yes. That's all I have to say today. Live like this isn't forever.

"

Live like this isn't forever.

I'm Woolf. I'm Plath. I'm Sexton. I'm Thompson.
I'm Hemingway. I keep getting stronger in the
broken places: the childhood molestation, the
Klonopin fixation, the scorpion venom, the death
wish I can't pull the trigger on. I wave farewell to
arms. I yank my head out of the guillotine. I start
carving away at the gangrene. I'm a fucking doctor.
I'm Dr. Death. I'm a cold-blooded killer. I snatch
the demons parading about my skull. I lop off their
heads, one by one by one. I stack their corpses in
the foyer like sand bags. I'm Lucifer, cutting jobs.
I'm God, clipping wings. I'm Ted Bundy, cuming all
over their dead bodies.